KT-499-785

# PET OWNER'S GUIDE TO THE
# GUINEA PIG

## Chris Henwood

RINGPRESS

# ABOUT THE AUTHOR

Chris Henwood has been keeping and breeding small animals for over twenty-five years. During this time he has been responsible for introducing several species and mutations to the pet fancy. He is an international judge of hamsters of all species, and is the author of numerous books and articles on all aspects of small animals and their care. He acts as an advisor to television programmes and to the RSPCA on small animal care. He keeps a varied collection of species at his West Sussex home which range from chipmunks and hamsters to a Shar Pei dog.

## Photography: Amanda Bulbeck.

Published by Ringpress Books Limited,
PO Box 8, Lydney, Gloucestershire,
GL15 6YD, United Kingdom.

First published 1999
©1999 Ringpress Books Limited. All rights reserved

No part of this book may be reproduced or transmitted in form or by any means, electronic or mechanical, including photocopying, recording, or by any information storage and retrieval system, without permission in writing from the publisher.

**ISBN 1 86054 110 0**

Printed in Hong Kong

UNIVERSITY OF LINCOLN
NOV 2002

# CONTENTS

# 1 Introducing The Guinea Pig

The guinea pig, or to give it its proper name, the Domestic Cavy, is one of the oldest and most widely kept of all the small pets. Its popularity is well founded. Guinea pigs are chunky, rather cheerful, little animals with very sociable, yet somewhat timid, natures. They are unable to jump or climb very high and are less likely to gnaw away at their hutches than most other rodents and rabbits. They may be kept in pairs, small families or single-sexed groups. They do not breed as often as other small rodents and, when they do, their litters are relatively small. They can be housed in a number of different ways both indoors and out, although they are somewhat more delicate than the rabbit.

The guinea pig is a member of the rodent family. Rodents are highly adaptable creatures with a worldwide distribution; variations of the species live in almost every corner of the earth. A feature common to all rodents is their ability to gnaw, and, indeed, that name is derived from *rodere*, the Latin for 'to gnaw'. They are relatively tolerant of most temperatures and environments.

## ORIGINS

It is sad that very little is known about our familiar guinea pig in the wild. In fact, we are not even sure exactly which species the Domestic Cavy has evolved from. Like the cat and dog, the guinea pig has been kept in captivity for such a long time that its history has been lost.

It is thought that the most likely ancestor is *Cavia aperea* which is found in South America. In the wild, this is a rather drab-looking animal. However, like the domestic animal, it has a stocky build, fairly short legs and short, unfurred ears. There are three digits on the hind feet and four on

*The guinea pig has its roots in South America.*

the front, all armed with sharp claws. These animals appear in a very wide range of habitats, including open grassland, forest edges, swamps and rocky areas.

They are usually found in small groups of from five to ten, generally made up of an adult male, two or three adult females and their offspring of various ages. They can be very vocal, in a similar way to the domestic guinea pig. These sounds include bubbly squeaks of excitement, chirps of anxiety and a tooth-chatter of threat.

They are part of a group of species that has not been very well studied in the wild and very little is known about them at all. For example, we are not sure if they live in one area or whether they roam from place to place. It is thought that the first domesticated guinea pig was kept by humans about 3,000 years ago.

## DOMESTICATION

When the Spanish Conquistadors arrived in Peru in South America, they found that the native Incas of the Andes had domesticated the

*The Incas sacrificed guinea pigs and they were eaten on special occasions.*

wild cavies and had, either by accident or design, produced a number of colours that varied greatly from those seen in the wild.

The Incas allowed these small animals to run around the floors of their homes and fed them on scraps from their own table, but they were not just pets; they were sacrificed and eaten on special occasions, as they still are today in many areas of the Andes. When they are prepared for cooking they look very like little pigs and, for this reason, the Spanish called them 'Cochinillo das Indas' or the 'Little Indian Pig'. The Incas, however, called them 'cui'.

It is not known how the 'guinea' was added but one theory is that the Spanish transported them to Guyana and from there the various merchants took them to Europe as pets for their children. Another theory is that the first animals to arrive in Europe were sold for a guinea, which is roughly about £1.05p today – a lot of money in those days.

## BEHAVIOUR

As far as can be gathered, the behaviour of the guinea pig has not changed all that much since it was domesticated. Generally, guinea pigs like to live in groups, as they then feel that there is safety in numbers. The more individuals a predator has to chase, the more likely it is to be confused and not make a successful kill.

Perhaps the best way to learn

*A sociable animal, the guinea pig, or domestic cavy, prefers to live in groups.*

about how your guinea pig feels is to break down its daily behaviour into small, easily recognised actions. One of the most common things you see a guinea pig do is the jump. This is really a jump for joy. They do this when they are in a happy mood. It is not at all unusual to see a guinea pig suddenly jump straight in the air from a standing start, just for the joy of it.

A guinea pig that is relaxed and happy will lie stretched out almost flat on the floor either of its cage, or outside on the ground in its run. It is obvious that they are comfortable and at ease when they do this. Guinea pigs will greet one another by touching noses and this is a very friendly gesture.

However, a stiff-legged gesture means that he, or she, is trying to exert dominance over another, and the animal will usually rise up with its legs very stiff. This stance is usually a warning of any advances by other animals and, if the intruder does not back off, a fight may well take place.

## VOCALISATION

Guinea pigs are extremely vocal animals and communicate with each other by a series of squeaks and grunts. Now, while I cannot pretend to be able to tell you exactly what they are saying to each other, I hope that the following will be of some help in understanding what the various noises your guinea pig makes mean to you.

The cooing of a guinea pig is an

*You can learn a lot about your pet by observing its behaviour.*

unmistakable sound. Guinea pigs generally use this sound to reassure each other that all is well, particularly mothers to young. If you are lucky, you may well find that your pet will do this to you. When this happens it really will mean that you have become part of the guinea pig family.

The sound that most people associate with the guinea pig is a squeak or whistle and it is one of those sounds that, once you have heard it, you will never forget. It is quite a high-pitched noise and can be quite piercing. It is generally used as a warning of danger between animals. But it is also used as a sound of pain, of fear, or a cry for attention, for example when they are aware that you are just about to feed them.

The sound of chattering teeth usually means 'stay away'. It is a warning that can extend to other guinea pigs and humans alike. Be warned, if you are not used to guinea pigs and one chatters its teeth at you. This may be one of the rare moments when a guinea pig will bite, usually from fear.

The last sound is a gurgling one that is rather difficult to describe but, again, once you have heard it there is no mistaking it. This is the sound of happiness and is often given when something pleases the animal, like special food, or the return to the colony of an old friend. It is also the sound made by a male when a new female is introduced to him. Pure happiness.

# 2 Making The Choice

When buying your guinea pig, and choosing from the many different varieties – and more about these later – it is always wise to go to a very good pet shop or, even better, a private breeder. This is not to say that you will be unable to obtain what you want from a pet shop; it is just that you are more likely to find the exact animal you require from a breeder. Please do not attempt to hunt around for a bargain or the cheapest animals available; good guinea pigs are not expensive. If you want your animals as pets rather than for show, it is best to buy them when they are between the ages of six and twelve weeks.

When you are obtaining a guinea pig for show purposes, its age is not as important as it is for a pet. Usually show animals will be tame and used to being handled. Some breeders of show animals, in fact, will not sell animals until they are 16 to 20 weeks of age, in case they improve for show. On the other hand, some breeders will sell adult animals that have been shown and won classes but are not required for their own breeding programmes.

## HOW MANY?

Since guinea pigs are very social animals by nature it is best to keep them in pairs or small colonies. Should you decide to have a pair, but do not wish to breed, it is best to select two animals of the same sex. Most authorities advise obtaining two females (sows), as two adult males (boars) will fight. Although this can be the case, I have found no problems about keeping two adult males together, provided a few rules are observed. They should have been raised together from an early age and they should have no contact with any females. Males will usually only fight over access to females

*If you do not wish to breed, select two guinea pigs of the same sex.*

and the smell of females nearby can, in some cases, lead to a fight.

This is not to say that a bachelor guinea pig is out of the question – far from it; a single male can be very happy, but he must have a lot more attention from his owner than those kept together.

## LIVING WITH OTHER ANIMALS

You should not keep guinea pigs together with other species, for example rabbits, although people are often advised that it is perfectly acceptable to do this. Rabbits and guinea pigs are very different animals and require different foods. Unlike rabbits, guinea pigs require a high intake of vitamin C. Rabbits can also be very aggressive animals, even to other rabbits, and I have known adult rabbits to attack and kill guinea pigs, even when they have been kept together for a long time. Any problems between the two species and the guinea pig will come off the worst. Some success has been achieved in keeping guinea pigs with dwarf rabbits but, even so, I have still found that the rabbit tends to chew the ears of the guinea pigs.

## ASSESSING A GUINEA PIG

When choosing a guinea pig, take a couple of minutes to watch it in its hutch or pen. Moving slowly and smoothly and avoiding any sudden movements, reach out

*Take time to assess behaviour and condition before making your choice.*

towards your chosen animal. If it is interested in and aware of your hand, although a little shy, chances are that it will tame well. Disposition does run in varieties, and some colours and coat types are much more highly-strung than others.

I have found that the Abyssinians can be very vocal, even more so than normal, and they love being talked to, but they do not like to be held and stroked as much as some of the smooth-coated animals do. I am inclined to feel that this is because of the quality of the coat and that, because the hairs stand on end, this may make the skin more sensitive.

Before actually purchasing your guinea pig it is important to handle it. Ask the person selling it to get it out of the cage for you. The animal should be alert, with nice bright, clear eyes, and it should be firm to the feel and not be skinny or thin. The nails should not be too long and the coat should be nice and thick with no bald or thin patches.

## HANDLING
The correct way to pick up a guinea pig is to place the hand across the shoulders of the animal with the thumb behind the front legs on one side. The fingers then fall naturally into place over the shoulders and across the back of

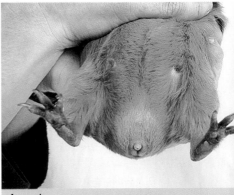

A male.

*The correct way to hold a guinea pig.*

A female.

the animal and are well forward, curling just underneath the ribcage.

The grip should be firm but not so tight as to squeeze the animal. The other hand should be placed under the animal's rump to give support for the remainder of the lifting.

Extra care must be taken when lifting a pregnant female.

### SEXING

Sexing guinea pigs at any age is a relatively easy thing to do, although I do admit that it is helpful if someone with experience shows you how, just once.

After lifting the animal, turn it onto its back. With its weight supported by the palm of the hand, put gentle pressure on either side of the genitalia. Moving the finger and thumb slightly apart will extrude the penis of the male cavy quite easily. The female, of course, has no such extrusion.

## SETTING UP HOME

There are many different types of housing for guinea pigs, both indoors and out. Some are better than others, but if you want your guinea pigs to be happy and healthy and to be with you for a long time, then they must be housed well. Unfortunately, a lot of the general pet shop hutches sold for guinea pigs are too small and often even made of metal or with a metal roof, which is most unsuitable. It is, therefore, important that, before you obtain your guinea pigs, you look around at the many different types and style of hutches and indoor cages that are obtainable.

## SITING THE HUTCH

The housing of guinea pigs is relatively easy. They do not require anything elaborate, but they do need adequate protection from variable weather conditions. I would suggest that, unless you can provide an extremely warm, weatherproof hutch (these are both difficult to obtain and usually very expensive) that you should site your cages or hutches in a wooden shed or in an outhouse. This should have adequate ventilation. Garages should not be used, unless they are unoccupied by cars, as the fumes are very

*Ideally, the hutch should be sited in an outhouse.*

dangerous and can easily kill guinea pigs in a very short space of time.

The advantage of having your animals under cover is that it makes looking after them a lot more comfortable for you and also provides protection from both draughts and damp for them. While guinea pigs do not need elaborate cages or hutches, these houses should not be shoddily built. They must be constructed so that they give good all-weather protection. No artificial heating of the shed should be necessary, but the shed should be weatherproof and draughtproof.

### INDOOR HUTCHES

As a general rule each animal requires 1860 sq cms of floor space and this area is also quite adequate for a sow with a litter. If your animals are together as a colony, they would be quite happy with a floor area of 930 sq cms each. Many breeders use large hutches, 40 cms high and 50 cms deep but of great length; these are then partitioned into suitable units to provide the required floor space for each group. If you decide that you would like to keep a greater number of guinea pigs and establish a breeding stud, then you

may wish to purchase block hutches; these are usually only available from specialist manufacturers and not generally for sale in your pet store.

Make sure the hutch has a front that can be totally removed, as this makes cleaning out much easier. A piece of wood about two inches high, fitted across the open front of the hutch, but removable for cleaning, will prevent the guinea pigs from falling out when the door is opened. This is known as a litter board. If your hutch is in a shed, the entire front may be of wire netting.

### OUTDOOR HUTCHES

If you cannot manage to keep the hutches in a shed or garage, or you need extra space, it may well be necessary to have outdoor hutches. Naturally these should be more substantial than the indoor type, well able to withstand the weather and giving protection to the animals at all times. They should have an extra separate sheltered nesting area, with an opening into the main part of the hutch to give the guinea pigs easy access. Remember that this gap should be quite wide so as to allow a pregnant female to get through if you are breeding them.

This nest area gives the animals somewhere to be warm in the winter and cool in the summer. The roof and the sides of the hutch should be covered in roofing felt so that the damp cannot get in. There should also be some form of shutter that can be fixed over the wire front at night and, in really bad weather, during the day. This shutter should leave about an inch clear at the top for ventilation.

## INDOOR HOUSING

There are also on the market a number of cages that have been designed to enable you to keep your guinea pigs in the house. Generally, these are very good and are extremely useful if you live in a flat, or only have a single animal that requires a lot more attention than a colony. They are also very useful as hospital cages for sick or old animals but, as they are small, the animals should be allowed out of the cage for exercise.

Indoor cages come in quite a few different types and over the past few years they have increased in style and size. However, they are all basically the same type, consisting of a plastic bottom and

*Indoor cages are becoming a popular option.*

a wire or clear plastic top, with a wire roof.

As with all small animals in the home, care should be taken about the location of the cage. Remember that, although guinea pigs like to see what is going on around them, they do not want to live in chaotic conditions. They dislike too much noise and loud music; they also have much keener hearing than we do and they can be affected by sounds that we do not hear. Therefore they should not be kept in a room with the television. A room that has some activity for at least part of the day is ideal, for example a utility room, providing it is not too sunny. A hall is also good.

Exercise can be provided by allowing the animal supervised outings from its cage around the floor. Be sure that the doors are closed and that people outside the room are aware that the animal is loose, or they may open the door just as your pet passes and hit it. Also ensure that other pets, for example cats and dogs, are under control.

## BEDDING AND LITTER

Bedding serves two purposes. It gives warmth and it soaks up urine, thereby keeping the guinea pigs clean. Some people start with a layer of newspaper then a top layer of wood shavings and sawdust. Recently some 'authorities' have stated that you should not use shavings for guinea pigs as they are allergic to them. All that I can say to this is that I, and many people that I know, have been keeping guinea pigs in this way for many, many years and I have yet to come across a single case of a guinea pig having an allergic reaction to shavings. However, because of the way in which some breeders interbreed animals year after year, it is quite possible that this has actually suppressed the animal's immune system and thus caused the allergy to occur.

I usually do not use newspaper without shavings, as I have found quite a few animals will eat the paper and, in some cases, the ink can cause quite a severe stomach upset. I supply each hutch with a good 10 cm (2 inch) layer of shavings and then top this off with a good amount of hay (see Chapter Three: Feeding your Guinea Pig). Do not use straw for guinea pigs as the sharp ends can be dangerous and easily get caught in their eyes, especially those of babies, as they burrow into it.

## OTHER EQUIPMENT

As guinea pigs are a grassland animal, unlike the burrowing rabbit and hamster, they are not so interested in toys as those other species, although they do still love a game. I have found that my animals are particularly fond of tubes and boxes in which they can hide. These, I think, make them feel safe and secure from their natural enemies. Take a cardboard box, cut a series of holes in the sides, and place the box on the ground. Sit back and watch the animals run in and out of the various holes. You will also probably find that they will decide to sleep inside the box as well. A large, permanent version of this can be made outdoors by using earthenware pipes, slightly buried into the ground of the guinea pigs' run.

## FEEDING BOWLS

Guinea pigs very often throw their food dishes around the hutches and, in some cases, will use them as toilets, so the best feeding dishes are those that are too heavy to be thrown, earthenware ones for example. Or you can buy plastic and stainless steel bowls that can be clipped to the wire front of the cage.

*Use a heavy, earthernware bowl which cannot be tipped up.*

## WATER BOTTLE

Water should be supplied in a gravity-fed bottle. Guinea pigs drink quite a large amount of water and it must be available at all times. I do not like the use of a bowl for water because, as stated above, some guinea pigs will use their bowl as a toilet, and this will obviously contaminate their water supply.

*A gravity-fed water bottle can be attached to the side of the cage or hutch.*

### OUTDOOR RUNS

In the summer it is possible to allow your cavies out on a grassed area in a suitably fenced area. The most suitable way to do this is to use what the pet stores call a run, but it is more correctly called a Morant. It was invented in the 19th century by a Major Morant for use by poultry and rabbits, but it is also very useful for guinea pigs. Basically, it is a hutch that allows the animals inside it to graze directly from the ground below. A true Morant consists of a triangular arc, two-thirds of which is covered with wire netting, the remaining third being covered by a wooden house. The whole of the floor area is also covered with large diameter wire netting to stop the animals from digging out (although this is rare with guinea pigs), yet still allow the grass to be grazed. To prevent fouling of any particular area, the hutch should be moved daily to a new patch.

A good-sized Morant is about 300 cms in length and 80 cms high. The house part should take

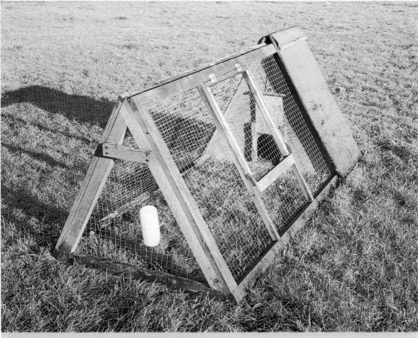

*An outdoor run will be appreciated during the summer months.*

up about one-third of the total length and should be made from good tongue-and-groove. Inside the house a raised shelf should be fitted to allow the animals to sleep on a dry surface should they so wish. This type of hutch is only meant for small groups of animals in good weather and should not be used in winter.

Naturally, outdoor runs should be located in an area of the garden that does not get too hot, or that has some shade. It should not receive the full midday sunshine. Guinea pigs love to sunbathe, but they do not want to get too hot, and white animals can suffer from sunburn, particularly on the ears. An area that gets the early morning or late afternoon sun is best.

### ARRIVING HOME
Remember that, when you bring your guinea pig home for the first time, it will need to settle into its new home. The sights, sounds and smells will all be different and perhaps quite frightening. Give the animal time to get accustomed to its new surroundings before you try to get to know it and show it off to the rest of the family.

Introducing a new animal to an established group can be very easy with guinea pigs. Just allow the established animal, or animals, into the area used for exercise and introduce the new guinea pig. Place plenty of food in with them and they will soon settle down. Once you are sure they are getting

*Give the new arrival a chance to settle before showing him off to friends and family.*

*If you are introducing a new guinea pig to an established group, make sure there is plenty of food around.*

on, they can then be placed in the sleeping area. On occasions, you will find that one animal will take a dislike to the newcomer. This is usually a dominant female, and she will probably chase the new animal around for a while. Do not worry about this unless you can see that the new animal is really getting bullied. If this is the case, take the two of them out and bath them. They will then both smell the same and the dominant female will usually accept the newcomer.

# 3 Diet & Nutrition

When you buy your guinea pig, it is a wise precaution to ask the seller what the animal has been feeding on. Then, if you wish to change the diet, you may do so gradually and thus not upset the digestion of the animal.

The essential items in the diet of the guinea pig are:

- Hay and water.
- Cereals in some form.
- Green and root foods.
- Occasional supplements.

## HAY

As with water, hay should be given freely at all times. Often people do not realise that guinea pigs are basically grazing animals and that, without hay, they find it very difficult to digest what they have eaten, whatever it may be.

On the whole, guinea pigs prefer soft meadow hay to the coarser type, but this may be used if the softer hay is not available. The smell alone will tell you if the hay is fresh. It should not smell of

*Hay, cereal and water are essential items in the cavy diet.*

mould, nor should it be dusty. Apart from its use as food, hay also provides a better source of warmth as bedding than anything else. As stated previously, straw should not be given to guinea pigs.

## WATER

Water should be provided at all times from a water bottle. Try to obtain one with a stainless steel tube as some animals will try to bite and chew the tube and, if it is not made of stainless steel, this can cause a lot of problems. Water should be changed daily.

## CEREALS

The major proportion of guinea pig owners give a basic diet of some form of seed and cereal mixture. Usually, this will contain crushed oats, wheat, barley, some form of maize and grass pellets and, occasionally, dog biscuits. In recent years, some companies have begun to add such items as locust beans, crushed peas and alfalfa, and these are all loved by most of my guinea pigs.

## GREEN FOOD AND VEGETABLES

There is often a debate by the various people that keep guinea pigs on a large scale as to whether or not guinea pigs really need 'wet' foods, as these are called, or whether they are all right on just a dry diet. All I can say is that my animals are fed on a mixed diet and I have found that they remain very happy and have, on average, a long lifespan.

Various green foods and vegetables may be fed to them, although a few do need to be used with a little thought. Therefore I have listed below a selection of the most commonly available foods and the problems, if any, that are associated with them.

### Lettuce

Although lettuce is the most common of the salad crops and is often 'saved' for the animals, it can be very dangerous if fed in large amounts. This is because it can cause a serious liver complaint. However, do not let that stop you from feeding it. Guinea pigs love it, but give it in small amounts only.

### Cabbage

Again, this can be a bit dangerous if overfed in any one meal. The outer leaves are the most beneficial, the inner leaves having much less food value, particularly

*A wide range of fruit and vegetables can be fed in moderation.*

in the white types. Cabbage can also have the effect of increasing the amount of urine produced by some guinea pigs.

### Cauliflower
This is, without a doubt, one of the most useful of all the green vegetables. It has a less dramatic effect on the system than the cabbage family. The leaves and stalks, which contain the best food value, are also the bits which are usually discarded by the cook. Guinea pigs seldom seem to refuse this item of food.

### Chicory
This is another very useful food, but it can be rather difficult to obtain in some areas. It is not only a good food but also contains a rather valuable tonic. This is also true of spinach, but this can be a very acquired taste for a lot of animals, so do not be surprised if your animals refuse this item in their diet.

### Sprouts and Spring Greens
These are very similar in all respects to the cabbage.

### Kale
A much overlooked vegetable to my mind, and my guinea pigs love this in all its forms. Like cabbage, it can cause an increase in the

amount of urine produced if fed in large amounts.

### Parsley

This is a perennial herb rather than a vegetable, but it will provide green food all year round, year after year. As with chicory and spinach, it can be an acquired taste.

### Root Vegetables

Almost all types of root vegetables, with the exception of potatoes, may be fed to guinea pigs; some are liked by all but others are an acquired taste. However, one that I have yet to see a single animal refuse is the carrot. All guinea pigs love these and they are a very useful food.

Guinea pigs also enjoy a number of other fruits and vegetables, for example apple, pear, celery, peas, bean sprouts and many more.

## FLOWERS AND WEEDS

The flowers of your garden can produce an amazing variety of foods for your guinea pigs. You can feed quite a large number of different flowers but you should always avoid the flowers and leaves of any bulbous plant, as these are usually poisonous to all livestock. Among the more commonly grown plants that may be fed to guinea pigs are marigolds, nasturtiums, phlox, asters, wallflowers, salvias, sweet peas, cornflowers and alyssum.

By far the easiest weed to obtain for your stock is grass. Guinea pigs just adore it. Many other weeds or wild flowers may be fed to your animals. However, they are not always that easy to recognise and a few are highly dangerous; for example, the buttercup is dangerous when fresh although it is okay when dried in hay. It is impossible for me to list all those plants that are suitable as there are so many, but below you will find a short list of the most common. If you do not know what a plant looks like, check with a good plant identification guide and do not pick plants if you are not sure what they are.

Plants that can be fed are burnet, cow parsley, coltsfoot, chickweed, crosswort, dandelion, dock, groundsel, hedge parsley, knot grass, mallow, nipplewort, plantain, shepherd's-purse, sow thistle, trefoil, vetch, watercress and yarrow. It is essential that you know what you are feeding to your animals so, if in doubt, leave it out.

*Food is enjoyed by guinea pigs, but beware of overfeeding.*

It is also important to remember that it is illegal to take a whole plant from the wild. Also remember, if you are collecting from an area other than the garden, to make sure that the area has not been sprayed with any chemicals or hormonal sprays or visited by animals.

## SUPPLEMENTS

Guinea pigs, together with primates including ourselves, are unable to produce their own vitamin C and therefore require it as an addition in their food.

In summer, if your guinea pigs are allowed plenty of green foods, they should obtain enough vitamin C, but in winter it is best to give some vitamin supplement. This may be given in the form of ascorbic acid tablets dropped into their drinking water daily, or rosehip syrup, or baby vitamins given either in the water or food.

You cannot overdose this vitamin as it is water-soluble and any excess will be excreted in the urine. You can, however, overdose if you give it in the form of cod-liver oil. As this is an oil, it is stored in the body and may cause paralysis. Should you wish to give some oil-based vitamin supplement then please ensure that it is in the form of a polyunsaturated oil.

### WHEN TO FEED

I would usually recommend that you feed your guinea pigs twice a day, with two separate meals – the dry cereal, along with the hay, in the morning, and the vegetables in the evening, along with a further addition of hay. Grass etc. may be given at any time. Do not store grass as it will start to heat up and will then be unsuitable to be fed at all. The amounts eaten will depend on each individual animal. For their size, guinea pigs can eat a vast amount of grass with no ill effects.

*Feed your guinea pig twice a day.*

# 4 Caring For Your Guinea Pig

The key to keeping guinea pigs in good health is feeding the correct diet and providing suitable housing, which must be cleaned out regularly.

## CLEANING OUT

When you clean out your guinea pigs I would suggest that you remove the animals to the play or exercise area and then get on with the cleaning out in peace – otherwise you will find that the area you are trying to clean is the exact area that your guinea pig wishes to sit on at that very point in time.

Remove all the bedding and the shavings and clean the hutch or cage thoroughly. It is a good idea, at least once a month, to wash the entire cage or hutch with a mild disinfectant solution. Special solutions that are safe for your animals but harmful to bugs can be obtained from most good pet shops. Once all the soiled material has been removed, then replace it with a good deep litter of shavings and nice big piles of hay. If the weather is very cold, providing the bedding is not wet on top, it can be covered with a fresh layer of shavings and hay. As mentioned before, *do not* use straw, as this can be very sharp and, when guinea pigs burrow into it, it can cut the eyes very badly.

If your guinea pig is housed inside, you will not have to use quite so much hay and shavings as you would outside, as the extra warmth will not be required.

You will probably find that you will need to clean out the indoor animals more often than those outside. Outside animals should be cleaned out at least once a week, while those indoors you may wish to clean out every other day.

## GROOMING

Generally, guinea pigs enjoy being

*Above: Accustom your guinea pig to being groomed from an early age.*

*Below: Long-haired varieties will need daily attention.*

groomed – carefully and lovingly brushed or combed. It not only helps the guinea pig to keep its coat clean, but it also gives you the opportunity for the early detection of vermin and any skin disorders. Young guinea pigs should be accustomed to grooming from a very young age, and four weeks is certainly not too young to start. As a general rule, long-haired animals will require grooming daily, while those with short coats, Abyssinian and Rex, will only require daily brushing when they are in moult in the spring and autumn.

## BATHING
In general, except for shows, there is no real need to bath young guinea pigs. Wash them only if they have become very muddy from an outdoor run, or if they are dirty from diarrhoea, or from giving birth or for other medical reasons such as skin mites, when a special shampoo should be used.

## HOLIDAYS
Do not forget that when you go on holiday you will have to find someone to look after the guinea pigs for you. With enough water, dry food and plenty of hay, a guinea pig can stay alone in its

*Hard feed, such as carrots, will help to wear down the teeth.*

hutch or cage quite happily for a day or two, but no longer. For a longer period you will need to have someone come to the house to look after the animal for you – not only to feed and water it, but to let it out into its exercise area and also to give it the cuddles and care that it is used to.

## TEETH

The guinea pig is a rodent and, as with all rodents, their teeth continue to grow throughout their lives. Normally the teeth are worn down by rubbing against each other, the top against the lower, and by wear and tear from the hard foods that they eat. Should, by any chance, these teeth become misaligned, through damage due to rough handling, a fall or a fight, then they will not wear as they are supposed to and will continue to grow. If this is allowed to happen, the teeth can eventually grow right into the animal's face. Misaligned teeth will require clipping at regular intervals, often as much as once a week. Cutting teeth is not painful for a guinea pig but he, or she, may not like the idea too much and may wriggle. It is a good idea to ask an

31

experienced guinea pig breeder to help, or your vet will be able to do the job for you. It is not a difficult thing to do, but you will need to be shown how by someone that is used to doing it.

Sometimes a guinea pig will break its front teeth in a fall or from chewing the wire of its hutch or run. They will easily grow again quite quickly but, until they do, if the break is uneven, they should be trimmed to an even length with nail-clippers. This should only be undertaken by an experienced cavy-keeper or a vet.

### NAILS

The nails of some guinea pigs never appear to need cutting at all while others require frequent

*Seek expert help if nails need trimming.*

trimming, particularly on the front feet where, sometimes, if you are not careful, they may grow right round and go into or under the foot.

In a light-coloured variety it is easy to see where to cut the claw as the pink quick is clearly visible, but on the darker varieties it is more difficult, so trim off only a little at a time until the nail looks a more comfortable length. If you should happen to cut too far and the nail bleeds, dip the claw in unperfumed talcum powder, which will stop the bleeding. If you are new to keeping guinea pigs, it would be wise to seek expert help from a breeder, or ask your vet to perform the task.

### TREATING GUINEA PIGS

Guinea pigs, when correctly cared for, are very healthy animals, rarely troubled with illness or accident. In years gone by, the general idea was that an ill guinea pig was a dead guinea pig. However, over the past few years, more and more has become known about the illnesses and diseases that guinea pigs can suffer from. Thus more and more cases of illness can be successfully treated. However, it is not unusual for a guinea pig that is ill to decide for itself that it is not going to get better and simply lose the will to live. Also, as with other rodents, guinea pigs are very good at hiding that something is wrong with them until it is too late for you to do anything about it.

## SIGNS OF ILL HEALTH

The question I am often asked is "How will I know if my animal is ill?" Well, the only answer to this is to watch and to get to know your animals. Once they have been with you for a while, you will soon learn that each one has a favourite place to sit or to lie in. One may run to the front of the cage when you feed it, another may run away when you get close. If these normal day-to-day rules change, then that is the time to look for a problem.

Ill guinea pigs often mumble to themselves, they will hold their head in a different way, their coat will not look so bright, and so on. If you are at all worried by the behaviour of your animal, take it to your vet. It is much better to have a false alarm and a healthy guinea pig, than to hold back and then have a very sick animal that the vet may not be able to do anything for.

## COMMON AILMENTS

Here are some of the main illnesses that can occur in guinea pigs. However, remember that, if you are in doubt as to what is wrong with your animal, then you must take it to your local vet. It may appear, from reading about these ailments, that there is a lot that can go wrong with a guinea pig. Far from it! You may keep animals for years and years and never have a single problem. Please do not let the thought of possible diseases and problems put you off keeping these great pets.

## INJURIES FROM FIGHTS

Usually an adult boar will live quite happily with an immature boar, but it is rare for two adult boars to live together successfully unless they have been brought up together, or are father and son, and they have not come into contact with females as adults. Should two adult boars be placed together you are very likely to have a serious fight on your hands. On occasion, sows may also fight, especially when a new group is placed together and they are establishing who is going to be the boss in the pecking order of the colony. Usually this is not serious; only very rarely do you

come across a particularly disagreeable sow who will make life a misery for the rest of the group. If you do, it is best to remove her and let her live either with just a single female that she will tolerate, usually a daughter, or with a boar.

The injuries from these fights are usually minor ones such as torn ears, which heal without much trouble. Bites on other parts of the body should be washed with a mild antiseptic solution and dabbed with antiseptic cream. Most guinea pigs will not bite humans deliberately, but be very careful if you are attempting to separate fighting animals – they may not realise that it is you they are biting and not their enemy.

## EYE INJURIES

It often happens, particularly with young animals, that a stalk of hay will poke them in the eye, causing the eye to become opaque. Usually this will clear in quite a short space of time. A small amount of eye ointment sold for humans will help. Always ensure that no small piece of stalk or grain husk is still in the eye.

## MOUTH SCABS

Occasionally guinea pigs will cut their lips and mouths on sharp food, then germs may enter this area and cause a sore. These are often difficult to cure. However, I have found that an old-fashioned remedy is great – try painting the wound with gentian violet, obtainable from chemists, although you will probably have to ask for it.

## LYMPHADENITIS

When feeding hay and fresh grasses to your animals, please be very careful that you do not include thistles. It is easy for your guinea pig to get a thistle thorn embedded in its throat. This will then set up an inflammation which can lead to a large swelling. This rarely bursts of its own accord and will have to be dealt with by the vet.

## ABSCESSES

These are occasionally caused by knocks or fights, or by items of sharp food. A fairly hard lump will be felt, usually on the throat or neck. It is best to leave this alone. If it is an abscess it will slowly grow, often to an enormous size, and will become softer when it is getting ready to burst.

The affected individual should be removed to a hutch or pen on its own, because, if the abscess does burst, the other guinea pigs may become infected by licking the wound. When it bursts, a lot of pus will come out. Wipe this away gently and wash the area of the abscess with either warm salt water or a mild antiseptic solution daily until the wound is healed.

## SKIN COMPLAINTS

The guinea pig seems to be particularly prone to various skin complaints. One of the most common is called by a number of different names, the most usual being Sellnick or Rat Mange. It is caused by a small mite burrowing under the skin surface. The first signs are tiny raised spots on the skin, which itself becomes scurfy, and the hair begins to fall out. These areas itch and so the guinea pig scratches itself. If your animal starts losing its hair and has scratch marks on its skin, this is probably the cause.

A few years ago there used to be a number of different types of human skincare products on the market that were suitable for you to bath your guinea pig in and which would cure them of this very quickly. Unfortunately, due to various regulations, almost all of these are not now available. You must, therefore, consult your vet if you notice the scratch marks.

## POSTNATAL SORES

After giving birth, sows often develop a sore on their back. This is usually due to a mineral protein

deficiency. To avoid this, in late pregnancy give the sows about a quarter of a teaspoonful of soya milk flour mixed with a little milk stirred into their food and sprinkle on wheatgerm and mineral salts.

Also, after they have littered, you will find sows with raw areas on the rump and under the belly.

This is not a vitamin problem; it is just the result of the sow pulling the hair out when she is cleaning herself up after the birth. It is probable that she had a long and perhaps difficult birth and, by the time that she got around to cleaning the blood up, it had dried on her coat and she had problems

removing it. If you notice it in time then it should be possible to sponge her clean and dab her dry. The area can also be rubbed with a mild oil to grease the skin and promote new hair growth.

## PREGNANCY TOXAEMIA

This usually occurs in sows in late pregnancy, but on occasion it may occur in other stock. An overweight sow in late pregnancy is extremely close to physiological breakdown and any extra stress can bring on toxaemia. In tests it has been found that all that is necessary to induce toxaemia is to withhold green foods. When a guinea pig is under stress, the liver overacts and vast amounts of stored fats enter the bloodstream at poisonous levels. The blood becomes too acidic, the kidneys work overtime trying to clear it and the animal suffers from kidney failure. They usually appear to have muscle spasms and go into a coma and die. Unfortunately little can be done at this stage, but, if you make sure your guinea pigs are fit but not fat before breeding, you may never encounter this.

## IMPACTED RECTUM

As guinea pigs, especially boars, get old you may well find they have a lump of faecal matter blocked in the rectum. The only thing that you can do is to squeeze it out gently with a soft tissue wad and clean the area with warm olive oil. It is a most unpleasant task to deal with, with a smell to match, but in old animals it is a problem that may well occur.

# 5 *Breeding A Litter*

**B**efore you embark on breeding your guinea pigs, even in a small way, you should ask the question "What will I do with the babies?" I know that guinea pigs do not have a great number of babies in a litter, but they do all require good loving homes and they can take up a good deal of time and space. Remember that just because you have a pet shop near by, this does not mean that they will want your animals. They may not, so check first. Also do not rely on schoolfriends and family to take the babies. They may not be the colour your friends like, or the sex that they want. You must be prepared to keep all the babies produced by any mating.

Do not breed from animals that are in any way unhealthy or sows that are overweight. You could start to breed your guinea pigs when the sow is six to eight weeks of age. However, it is much better for the health of both the mother and the offspring to wait until she is at least twenty weeks of age. Having said this, you also do not want to leave it too long after this age to breed. Why?

## WHEN TO BREED

As a general rule, with most animals it is inadvisable to breed from young females who may have reached puberty, but who are too immature in their own behaviour to deal correctly with their own young. The same applies if they are physically immature and the pelvis has not reached an adequate size to prevent pain and difficulty during the actual birth. This is known as dystocia. The case of the guinea pig is rather different, however, because there is a greater risk of dystocia if the guinea pig does not have her first litter while she is still young. Once fully mature, the pelvic bones fuse, leaving her with

*Great care must be taken when selecting breeding stock.*

a rigid, perhaps undersized, pelvis and this may cause a difficult birth. It is for this reason that a first litter should be produced before a sow is one year old. The litter will then be born before the two halves of the pelvis fuse together. Subsequent births should be trouble-free.

## MATING

You can run more than a single sow with a boar, up to four, or even more, providing that you have a large enough run or hutch, and that you can provide homes for all the offspring produced. A sow will come into season once every two weeks and this will last a few hours. On some rare occasions, a sow may take a dislike to a boar and will refuse to mate with him. In this case you will have to mate her to a different boar. Sows are usually left with a boar for several weeks so it is not always possible to tell exactly when they have mated. The usual length of pregnancy, or gestation, is 65-72 days. Therefore, if you count 65 days from the day that they were first put together, that is

*An agouti boar: If you have enough room, four or more sows can run with a single boar.*

the earliest day that you can expect a litter.

## THE PREGNANT SOW

You must always be very gentle when handling pregnant, or 'in pig' sows. To lift them from their hutch, use both hands and give some support to the belly with your fingers. As they get near to their time to give birth, you will be amazed just how big a sow can get. You will begin to think that if she gets any bigger she will burst. Do not worry; this large size is quite common and is due to the fact that baby guinea pigs are born quite well developed.

About 48 hours before the birth you can feel that the pelvic bones are opening, ready for the birth. Litters can be of any number from one to six or more, although three appears to be the most common number. Sows only have two nipples with which to feed their young, but they usually manage to raise four or five babies quite well.

If the sow is still in with the boar when she litters, he will not harm the babies deliberately, but the sow comes into season again an hour or so after the birth and he will try to mate her; therefore the babies may be injured in the scuffle of mating. This is not really fair on the sow, as it greatly adds to the strain on her, not only feeding a litter but also carrying another as well.

41

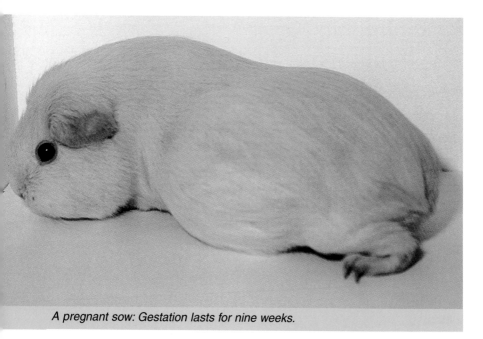

*A pregnant sow: Gestation lasts for nine weeks.*

On rare occasions, if two sows that are due to give birth share a hutch and one of them litters, this may excite the other female so much that she will abort her litter. Although this is rare, it is often best to remove the sow to a hutch either on her own or with a non-pregnant female. She may always be returned to the others after a week or so.

A non-pregnant female is a useful addition, especially if she has had litters of her own, as she will help the mother to clean and care for the litter as the babies are being born.

## DIFFICULT BIRTHS

I can assure you that 99.9 per cent of all guinea pig births are perfectly normal, so much so that often the first thing that you know about it is the sight of the babies running about when you go to feed the mother in the morning. I say in the morning, as most guinea pig mothers appear to prefer to litter at night. However, there are rare occasions when your sow will have problems. One of the most common causes of this is a large litter. Unfortunately, there is no way that you can prevent this.

What must you do if one of your sows has difficulties? If the baby's head is protruding, you can grip it gently with a clean cloth and very carefully ease it out. Do not pull too hard or you may cause a prolapse of the female's uterus. If the baby's head has not appeared and the mother is in obvious difficulties, you can insert your little finger and hook your fingernail on to the baby's teeth and then gently ease it out. If it is a breech birth, you may be able to make it move to the correct position by gently massaging the abdomen of the sow in a circular motion. If you are at all nervous about doing this, then you must take the animal to the vet at once.

## LARGE LITTERS

Litters over four may be split up and fostered quite easily on to sows that only have one or two babies of their own. Usually this is most successfully done when the babies are only a few days old. It is much more difficult if there is an age gap of more than a few days between the two litters, as the older babies will tend to push the younger ones aside.

To introduce the litters, rub some damp sawdust from the foster mother's hutch onto the baby. If the mother starts to fuss and lick it then she will usually accept it. However, if she will not, she will keep pushing it away, grind her teeth at it and may, on

A sow will often foster a baby from another litter, provided the youngster is a similar age (and a similar smell) to her own.

*The sow will need a peaceful environment when feeding her litter.*

rare occasions, bite it. If this is the case, then the baby must be returned to its mother, she will not mind the smell of the other female's hutch on her young. If a group of females are kept together and produce litters together you will often find that confusion is caused, and even the mothers will not know which baby belongs to whom and will feed any youngster that attempts to suckle.

**HAND-REARING**

If the babies do not appear to be getting enough food, or if the mother should die and you are unable to foster them with another female, you can either supplement their milk intake or hand-rear them. Use an eye-dropper and feed a milk powder mixed with a little warm water and glucose solution. You should feed them every two hours, at least, for the first day or so; ideally this should be through the night as well, but often one feed at night is enough.

They soon become adept at sucking at the dropper but do not squeeze the milk into their mouths or they will choke; let them take it at their own pace, about one eye-dropper full each at first and then increase this to whatever they will take. In addition to this, it is always best to put a mixture of bran, together with a little brown bread soaked in milk, in a shallow dish so that they can get accustomed to helping themselves. Once they get the idea, keep this dish clean and freshly filled each day and stop dropper feeding, except for any small individuals.

## WEANING

Babies are usually fed by their mothers for four weeks or so, at which point they should be separated into their different sexes. Young males will tolerate each other until they are about 12 to 16 weeks old, then they will usually start to become aggressive to each other; chattering their teeth is a sure sign of aggression. An adult boar will usually tolerate a young boar as company, if he has been on his own, but he will not tolerate a young boar if there are females about.

## HOW MANY LITTERS?

Do not allow your sow to have more than three litters in one year and do not allow her to become fat when she is not with a boar, as this will also cause problems. Most sows will stop breeding at three to four years of age, although some will stop before this and some will go on after. The average lifespan

*The babies are now four days old.*

*At ten days old, the babies look like mini replicas of their parents.*

of a guinea pig is five to six years.

I would not advise you to allow sows to litter between December and March. It is during this period of the winter that animals are at their lowest and food is beginning to deteriorate due to storage. Feeding a pregnant sow during the winter months requires a little more thought than feeding one at other times of the year, or one that is not pregnant.

She must not be allowed to become fat but, at the same time, she must eat enough, not only to provide for herself, but also for her unborn babies. She must be given plenty of fresh vitamin C-bearing foods as well as her daily dry food diet.

## BREEDING RECORDS

If you are keeping guinea pigs with the aim of showing them, detailed records should be maintained for each animal. It is most important that a breeder can see at a glance which animal has been bred from which individual, and which combination of animals produces the best results.

By far the simplest way of doing this is to give each animal a card. This card can then be stored in an index box. You should record such information as the name of the animal, its parents, grandparents, colour, age, the date of all litters borne or sired by it, the size of the litters and their sex and colour. Then, from the information that is contained on the cards, detailed pedigrees can be produced and, should a rare variety be produced, its ancestry can then be traced back and it may be possible to produce another by the same means.

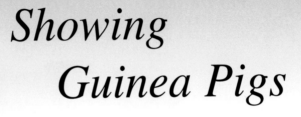

# 6 Showing Guinea Pigs

Should you decide that you would like to show your guinea pig, the first thing to do is to go along to one of your local shows. You will find that these shows are often advertised in your local paper or displayed on the notice-board of your pet shop. A lot of the country shows in the summer months will have either a fur and feather show or a display tent in which you will be able to gather information on local breeders. Talk to the local breeders and try to decide which variety you would like to keep. If you already have a guinea pig that you believe may be worth showing, take it along and ask one of the fanciers what they think of it.

There are a number of clubs that you can join both locally and nationally. Should it be a specialist club, then this will probably be a national one but, even so, most of these clubs will join with local clubs and hold local events.

The advantages of showing, apart from the enjoyment that you will get from it, are more obvious to the experienced breeder than the beginner. You will meet other breeders and you will be able to show just how good you are at keeping and breeding the variety of guinea pigs that you have chosen. You will not win a great deal of money as the prizes are small but you may well win a cup or, at least, a rosette.

## COAT TYPES AND COLOUR

Guinea pigs have, over the many years that they have been retained as pets, been developed into a large number of varieties that affect both the coat type and colour. Basically there are four major types:-

1. Smooth
2. Abyssinian
3. Long-haired
4. Rex

A large variety of colours and coat types have been developed. This is a Curly Long-haired Texel.

In the fancy, as the owning of a pet species that is shown is called, the different types of guinea pigs are divided into two different divisions. These are known as the Self Varieties, which feature all the smooth-coated guinea pigs of a single colour and the Non Self, which covers all the other varieties in all coat types including one-colour long-haired, Rex and Abyssinian coated. In all of the fancies each variety must conform to a Standard as closely as possible if they are being exhibited.

## WHAT IS A STANDARD?

Each of the different varieties has what is known as a Standard. This is simply a description of what a perfect guinea pig of that variety should look like.

The descriptions I am giving of each variety are not the exact Standards, as these are all very similar and would prove very boring to quote. However, I hope that they will make you wish to learn more about each different variety.

If you find that you are particularly interested in one variety then it is well worth going along to a show and asking the show organiser to introduce you to a person who breeds, or knows about, this particular variety.

## SELF VARIETIES

Self variety guinea pigs are of a single colour only and this is important to bear in mind. They are all short-haired. Type is considered a very important feature of these animals.

Self guinea pigs should have a broad head with a relatively short face and bold, bright, quite large eyes. The petal-shaped ears should droop and must, obviously, be undamaged, showing no signs of a slight tear or wound for example. It can be an extremely difficult thing to assess type as well as colour in young animals before they reach maturity. Their bodies may well seem rather long compared with the desirable shape of an adult which is described as 'cobby'.

The actual coat should be relatively fine and this is often better in the sows than the boars. You will, for this reason, often find that a sow is a higher winner than a boar. In some colours the head of the sow also tends to be a better shape than that of the boar.

Also, while the smooth-coated pet guinea pig does not really require any large amount of grooming, this is an important part of the life of a show animal. Grooming is essentially by hand, although some exhibitors prefer to rub a piece of silk along the natural lie of the fur to give a final gloss to the individual's coat. Grooming should be done on a regular basis, not only just before a show. You can groom out the longer guard hairs by drawing your thumb and forefinger along them, then rub from head to rump with your hands.

This can be difficult to get the hang of at first and I would ask to be shown how to groom when you purchase your animals, even if they are only young.

## SELF BLACK

This is probably the most popular of all the self varieties. It is a deep, glossy black. Some individuals may be

*Self Black: A deep, glossy colour.*

somewhat spoilt by having odd reddish hairs in the coat, while white markings are another serious blemish. Self Blacks must also have a matching undercoat that is black to the skin.

## SELF WHITE

The pure albino form of this variety is characterised by its red eyes. There is, however, also a dark-eyed variety which often retains some pigment so that its ears may be dark. The Dark-Eyed White presents a much greater challenge for exhibition purposes since, although pigmentation on the body and feet may be removed by selective breeding, eye coloration often suffers accordingly. The head of the variety also tends not to be as

*Self White: Note the ruby red eyes.*

good as that of the Pink-Eyed variety.

As with all pale-coated varieties, it is vital to keep these animals under spotless conditions in order to minimise the risk of dirty marks on their fur. However, in both varieties, fur may well yellow with age and this is not a fault of care conditions, just a fact of life.

## SELF CREAM

This variety usually has exceptionally good type and shape. It has dark ruby eyes that can look almost black in certain lights and which, to my mind, set off the cream colour to perfection.

The Standard actually calls for a pale even colour, with an undercolour to match and must be free from any lemon or yellow tingeing. However, there are a

*Self Cream: A pale, even colour is required. This animal has a satin coat.*

number of different shades of Cream throughout the fancy, from almost apricot to off-white, and different breeders and judges prefer different shades. It should actually be the colour of the cream at the top of a bottle of Jersey milk, if you can still find such a thing. Basically a dark Cream is too like the Buff, while the lighter Cream looks like a badly-stained White.

Skill in breeding is also rather necessary as litters tend to contain different shades of cream and you cannot just breed any colour shade to any other. Care must be taken; it is best to breed dark to light to maintain a fairly even colour.

## SELF GOLDEN

This is yet another colour variety whose colour varies greatly from a brassy yellow to an almost pale red. There are actually two varieties, as with the Self White and Self Black – Red and Black-Eyed.

The ideal colour lies between the above-mentioned ends of the colour range. It should be a rich, almost ginger, colour with undercoat matching the colour of the top coat. As with the Self White, the Black-Eyed variety tends to be more difficult to breed without losing the eye colour along with unwanted skin pigmentation.

51

*Self Chocolate: This should be a rich, dark shade.*

## SELF CHOCOLATE

The Self Chocolate should be a rich dark chocolate (not a pale milk chocolate) with eyes to match. Their biggest fault is undoubtedly colour and, as often as not,

the presence of white or golden hairs, particularly on the belly. The type has improved over recent years but it is not a top standard variety.

## SELF RED

Over recent years, this variety has declined to a great extent, with quality show stock being rather scarce.

The colour should be a dark, rich mahogany red, with matching ears and feet. The eyes are a deep ruby red. Young animals of this variety will become lighter as they grow older, so the darkest animals should be kept for exhibition purposes, assuming, of course, that their type conforms.

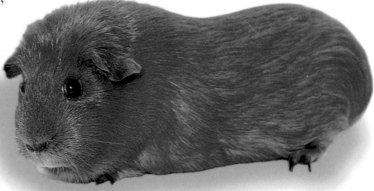

*Self Red: Mahogany red with matching ears and feet.*

*Self Beige: A pale chocolate with red eyes.*

A few white hairs in a young Self Red need not necessarily cause concern. These may well be replaced as the animal grows, leaving solid coloration, and some breeders claim that the individuals showing a trace of white produce offspring with the better coloration. The change of this coloration may not take place until the animal is approximately six months of age.

## SELF BEIGE

The Self Beige is actually the pink-eyed dilution of the Self Chocolate – basically a pale chocolate with red eyes. The Standard, to my mind, does not give a very good guideline to this colour although,

I admit, it is a very difficult colour to describe. It is a pale beige biscuit colour with a pink tinge. The actual colour varies greatly and you will find many different shades even in the same litter, from very dark to very light.

Breeders of this lovely colour usually advise that dark sows are used for breeding with a light boar or vice versa. If the top colour is okay you usually do not have to worry about the undercolour, as the colour goes right down to the skin.

## SELF LILAC

There is a similarity between the Self Lilac and the Self Beige, but the former should be a medium

53

*Self Lilac: There is a similarity between the Self Lilac and the Self Beige.*

shade of dove grey, without any trace of beige in its coat.

The Self Lilac is, in fact, a dilute form of the Self Black and, again, should have pink eyes. Coloration tends to fade as the young animals mature. The rules for breeding the Self Beige also apply to this variety.

## OTHER SELF VARIETIES

In some countries certain colours are recognised that are not known, or rarely known, in the UK. Among these are the Red-Eyed, Orange and Blue. There are also colours in the UK that are new to the show benches and are in small numbers and being worked on very hard by breeders to get them to show standard. Among these are the Buff (see rare varieties).

# 7 The Non Self Varieties

The Non Self Varieties can be short-haired and not one-colour, or they can show different coat characteristics, in which case they can be one or self-coloured.

## THE ABYSSINIAN

This is a coat variety, usually referred to by its owners as the Abby, and is probably one of the most popular and well-known of the Non Self varieties. This may be because it requires much less show preparation than other varieties. It is a rosetted, rough-coated animal, often confused with the Peruvian, which I shall be dealing with later, and which is, in fact, a long-coated mutation of the Abby.

The rosettes and ridges of the coat are formed in an unusual way and this is the most important point in

Abyssinian Roan: The Standard calls for the correct formation and positioning of rosettes.

a show Abyssinian. The ideal Abby should have four rosettes in a straight line over the saddle of the body, four around the rump and one or two on each shoulder. Where the hair growing in one direction from one rosette meets the hair growing in the opposite direction from another rosette, it forms a ridge. The rosettes should be so placed that the ridge runs in straight lines, both across the body and down the back and sides. The rosettes themselves should be deep, with hairs radiating from a pin-point centre. The coat should be harsh and there should be no flat smooth coat anywhere, and this includes the head.

The Abby has the appearance of having a Franz Josef moustache. There are a number of faults in the Abby and usually you can tell these at birth; for example, out-of-line or double-centred rosettes, uneven ridges, soft or long coat, although young animals' coats are often softer than they will be as adults. Understandably therefore, the Abby is not an easy animal to produce for show standard.

Colour is not considered a significant feature in this variety, but all-white animals are generally not popular as they tend to have very soft coats and this can be the case for all the one-coloured animals, for example Black and Red. Tortoiseshells, Roans and Brindle varieties tend to be the most popular for show as their coats tend to be harsh and stiff.

Abyssinians are lively individuals, some are often rather nervous and the boars are often rather aggressive toward other boars, more so than in other varieties, so it is important that this variety be handled very well to ensure that it remains tame.

Show preparation is important for the Abby but not so much as for the other varieties. A toothbrush makes a useful, suitably-sized grooming aid. Choose one with natural bristles if at all possible, to reduce the likelihood of static charge in the coat, as this will cause it to lie incorrectly. Giving the animals an occasional bath is also recommended by some exhibitors.

## THE DUTCH

The Dutch Cavy is a smooth-coated animal that is basically a white animal augmented by colour. The most common of the various colours is the Red and Black but it also occurs in Chocolate, Golden, Cream, Tri-colour and even Agouti.

*Dutch Red: A striking variety.*

It is a very, very distinctive variety. The rear part of the body should be coloured and the front white, with the demarcation line round the body being as near to the front legs as possible, without the colour being present in the front legs themselves. This is known as the saddle. The hind legs should have white socks of equal length going halfway up to the first joint and having straight demarcation lines round the foot. These socks are

*Dutch Black: The markings on either side of the face should be identical.*

known as stops.

The markings on the face should be as round as possible, including the eyes and ears and reaching to the whiskers, but not actually including them. The colour should not run on to the neck or under the chin, and the markings on either side of the face should be separated by a wedge-shaped blaze of white, extending up the centre of the face to between the ears. The markings on each side of the head and body should, ideally, be identical, giving a well-balanced appearance. Naturally this is the ideal and few actually achieve this.

Most Dutch, even some of the top winners on the show bench, have a few minor faults, the most common of these being cheek markings covering the whiskers and stops being too short or too long, or even no stops at all. Flesh-coloured markings on the ears are another major problem. Ears should be coloured both inside and out. Eyes should match the Standard for the coloured portion of the body.

As you may have gathered, it is very difficult to breed a perfectly marked Dutch animal and it is because of this that a lot of Dutch animals are usually available at shows. In order to breed a good animal you must buy good breeding stock. For this, it is important that you contact a good, top winning breeder of this variety and, in some cases, be prepared to pay more money than you may in other varieties. Having said this, you are unlikely to have to pay an awful lot of money even in this case. I have known a top winning animal to be sold at a show for a lot less than the prices charged in a pet shop for a normal pet type of guinea pig.

## AGOUTI

The typical ticked appearance of the Agoutis results from two distinct shades existing on each hair, thereby creating a banded effect linked with plain colours. The most popular colours are the Golden and the Silver, but there are a few other varieties, although these are not as popular.

## GOLDEN AGOUTI

This is the most commonly seen; it has a Black ground colour ticked with Golden and has a Golden belly colour.

## SILVER AGOUTI

This is one of my personal favourites of all the various varieties of guinea pigs. The

*Silver Agouti: Blue/Black ticked with Silver/Grey.*

ground colour is a Blue-Black ticked with a Silver-Grey. The belly is a dark Silver-Grey.

## CINNAMON AGOUTI

Probably the most commonly seen of the rare varieties of the Agoutis, the ground colour is a light Chocolate ticked with Silver and a dark Cinnamon belly colour.

## LEMON AGOUTI

This is a common Agouti colour among pet owners, but is rather looked down upon by the 'true' Agouti fanciers. Two varieties are possible; a Black-based and a Chocolate-based (also sometimes referred to as the Chocolate Agouti). Both have cream ticking and a creamy-yellow belly colour.

## ORANGE AGOUTI

This is a rare colour but it is becoming more common in the USA. It is similar to the Golden but has a Chocolate ground colour rather than the Black of the Golden.

## OTHER RARE AGOUTIS

It is also possible to produce Agoutis in dilute colours, for example Beige/Golden and Lilac/Cream. These have pink eyes and are, therefore, not regarded as true Agoutis but rather Argentes and in the UK are usually catered for by the Rare Varieties Section. We will come to these later.

The major faults with the Agouti guinea pigs are long, coarse, guard hairs which spoil the appearance of the ticking; uneven grooming which often leaves large dark patches on the coat; eye circles (a circle of lighter-coloured hair around the eyes); feet and belly that do not match the body colour and single, rather than Agouti-coloured, patches.

## TORTOISESHELL AND WHITE

A Tort and White, as this variety is more commonly known, is a smooth, short-coated guinea pig, with a patchwork colour of red, black and white. Each patch should be as square as is possible, with straight demarcation lines between each patch. The opposing patches on each side of the body should be of a different colour. The demarcation line between the sides should run in a straight line from the tip of the nose, between the ears, down the centre of the rump, between the legs, down the centre of the belly and under the chin to the nose again.

It is probably the most striking and beautiful of the guinea pigs and yet also one of the most heart-breaking to breed. The reason for this is that you may well breed more than a hundred animals without breeding one single show standard individual, no matter how good your foundation stock is. On the other hand, you could obtain two almost perfect individuals in a single litter. It is for this reason that you often find that Tort and Whites are kept by

*Tortoiseshell and White: A patchwork of red, black and white.*

fanciers who have a lot of room for keeping guinea pigs in large numbers. This has never been a variety that I have kept as more than a pet, but most Tort and White breeders that I have spoken to tend to agree that the major faults to avoid when buying breeding stock are:

1. Breeching: this is when one colour runs right around the rump.
2. Banding: a band of one colour going part or all the way around the body.
3. Brindling: patches of hairs of intermingled colours.

So, look for breeding stock with clean-cut patches of colour, even if it is cut in the wrong place. A nice straight belly line, even if it is uneven on the top, also appears to be very important.

## HIMALAYAN

As in other fancies, the Himalayan guinea pig has a white body with darker points These points should be either Black or Chocolate, and it can be very difficult to actually distinguish between the two shades, since the Black is equivalent to a dark plain chocolate while the Chocolate is paler. Also, the depth of the coloration can vary depending on the temperature; the ears are perhaps the most reliable means of separating the two different shades.

*Himalayan: A white body with dark points.*

The serious breeders of this variety will often go to considerable lengths to ensure that their animals have points of good colour. In order to achieve this, they will not allow them into the outdoor runs in the summer, as the sun is likely to make the animals too hot and this will cause the points to fade. A cool outhouse is the other option, or a hutch in a very shaded spot if they are outdoors.

Young Himmys, as they are called, will not develop their full colour until they are six or seven months old. They are born pure white, and the darker points emerge gradually as they get older, the pads being the first of the points to turn dark.

The points are the nose, usually referred to as the smut, which should be as large as possible, with the colour extending up the nose to between the eyes and down into the whiskers. The smut is very important because, for show judges, this is the vital area. The ears should be a matching colour and, as with all varieties, nicely dropping. The colour on the legs

*American Crested: Self-coloured with a crest of contrasting colour.*

must go well up the leg but not beyond the hock.

The show life of the Himalayan is rather restricted, due to the fact that, as mentioned above, the colour often does not appear until the animals are over six months. Again, as full-grown adults, the intensity of the colour on the points tends to fade.

Faults to look for in young stock of this variety are white toes or toenails, white patches on the feet, flesh-coloured ears or patches on the ears. Some also have dark rumps and these will usually be retained as adults. They will not be suitable for showing but do not discard these animals, particularly if they are sows, as they are useful breeders. Discard only those with the white feet.

Lastly, do not expect Himmys to be big guinea pigs; they are a naturally small variety and the Chocolate more so than the Black.

## CRESTED

This is not an old variety but, in its short life, it has gained great ground. As a variety, it originally occurred in the USA and was

Black Dalmatian: A black head with a spotted body.

introduced to the UK by the breeder Isobel Turner in 1972 when she imported six animals from Canada.

The crest is on the head in a form of a rosette, situated centrally above the eyes, but below the ears. The hairs of the crest radiate from a central point. Apart from the crest, the animal should be a smooth-coated individual. There are two basic types of Crested, the English and the American.

The English Crested is a Self-coloured animal with the crest the same colour as the body.

The American Crested is a Self-coloured animal with a crest of a contrasting colour. Probably the most popular American Crested are the Golden and the Black.

### ROANS AND DALMATIANS

Although these two different varieties are not related, they have a joint club and are usually classed together at shows.

The smooth Roan was developed, after many years of selective breeding, by Jan Belling. At first, it was basically a black animal with white hairs evenly mixed throughout the body. Over the years other breeders have managed to breed other colours in the Roan, for example, a Strawberry Roan, i.e. the combination of red and white hairs. Solid colour should be confined to the head and feet but white whiskers are not penalised.

Dalmatians are a spotted variety and accepted in any Self or Agouti colour. It actually evolved from a mutation of Self Blacks and was originally bred by Elizabeth Wilson.

The Dalmatian should have a black, or corresponding colour, or silvered head, with a blaze, eyes and coloured or silvered feet, to match the head.

Faults include the lack of a blaze, and spotting which is too heavy, uneven or too light.

Some difficulties arise if Roan are bred to Roan or Dalmatian to Dalmatian. This usually results in about one in four of the babies being born with small, practically non-existent eyes. In colour they are pure white and are known as Micropthalmic White. They also tend to have teeth problems and rarely live more than a few weeks. In order to avoid this situation, Roans and Dalmatians should be bred to the Self-coloured animals. For example, a Black Dalmatian should be mated to a Self Black animal.

# 8 *All Other Varieties*

## LONG-HAIRED VARIETIES

### PERUVIAN

This is probably the most spectacular of the various long-haired varieties of guinea pig. More care and attention must be given to the Peruvian than to any other guinea pig variety. It is a full-time occupation to breed and show Peruvians. Please believe me when I say that this is not a beginner's guinea pig. As an owner of this variety you must be prepared to brush and rearrange the long hair every day. Anyone contemplating this breed should join the Peruvian Cavy Club, who will give information on the do's and don'ts.

Genetically, the Peruvian is a Long-haired Abyssinian. The rosetting makes the hair on the top of the body lie towards the head and fall over the face, while the hair at the

Peruvian: In this variety, the hair grows towards the ears.

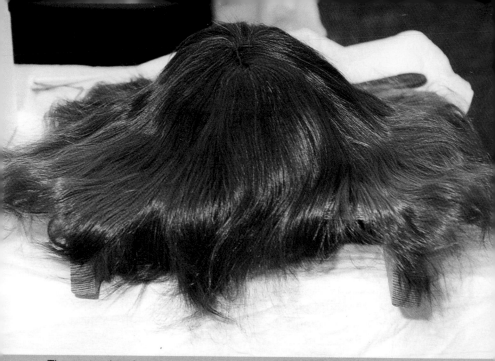

*The coat rather than the colour is judged on the show bench.*

rear end falls over the hindquarters, making it difficult to tell which end is which. Not all Peruvians have the temperament to sit still on their special show stands, as they are required to when being judged. The reason they have these special stands is so that they do not spoil their long coats, which may well grow up to 50 cms (20 inches) or more.

When Peruvians are born they are short-coated and should have two rosettes sited on the rump, but the hair does not grow towards the rump but towards the ears. Only the hair below the rosettes grows downwards. As the animal ages, the hair will start to part up the middle and should be encouraged downwards on each side of the parting. Eventually the hair is brushed over the two rosettes into what is called a sweep and, when long enough, at about 12 weeks of age, it is taken up into what is called a wrapper, made of paper and a small piece of balsa wood, and secured with a rubber band. At about five to six months of age, the side hair is also placed into wrappers, one on each side of the body. This is where the problems begin as these are inclined to come out rather easily; although, having said this, as the hair gets longer they are easier to keep in.

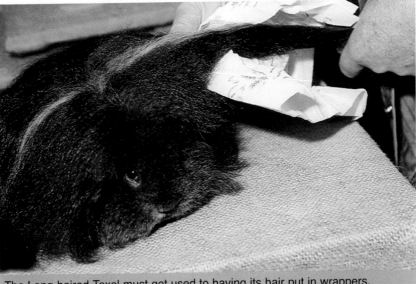

The Long-haired Texel must get used to having its hair put in wrappers.

If a Peruvian cavy objects very strongly to having the wrappers in and will not sit still, you might as well give up on that particular animal for show. Obviously the keeping of the animals in wrappers is only for show animals. Breeding stock, and those kept purely as pets, should have their coats clipped, but care should still be taken, as they do need to be brushed and bathed because the coats can quickly become matted even when clipped.

Peruvians, unfortunately, do show an abnormal tendency to chew their own fur, which can ruin the potential of a show animal. A constant supply of hay may help to prevent this habit.

The colour of a Peruvian does not matter, as it is the coat that is the most important factor on the show bench.

## SHELTIE

The Sheltie, like the Peruvian, is a long-haired animal and also needs a lot of care and attention. The difference between the two is that the Sheltie is the long-haired variety of the smooth guinea pig. The Sheltie's hair flows backwards, leaving the head clear, and forms a long train at the rear of the animal. Baby Shelties look quite different from the powder puff baby of the Peruvian. They look

Coronet: A combination of the Crested and the Sheltie.

the same as the smooth, short-coated varieties, but their coats grow quite quickly. It is necessary to train them in the same way as the Peruvian and, as with the Peruvian, I would suggest that you join the Sheltie Cavy Club. Some people only place wrappers in the train of a Sheltie, while others tend to also place wrappers in the sides; this will depend on the length of coat of the individual animal. As with the Peruvian, non-show Shelties should be clipped.

**CORONET**
The Coronet is basically a combination of the Crested and

Rex: The coat is short and dense, with the guard hairs standing upright.

the Sheltie and should be treated in the same way as a Sheltie.

Breeders are now also combining the Peruvian and Sheltie/Coronets with the Rex-coated animals and creating new Rex-coated Long-haired specimens.

These tend to have shorter coats than the pure Long-haired and are a little easier to care for.

## COAT TYPES: REX AND SATIN

The Rex-coated cavy is, to my mind, the best. I just love this variety. The coat appears woolly; this is because the guard hairs of the normal coat are very much shortened. This, in turn, has the effect that the coat will not lie flat but will curl and stand upright. The coat should be dense and short. Any colour is permissible.

Rex bred to Rex will breed true, but bred to a Self coat you will only obtain Selfs, although some of these will be carriers and these are useful for breeding.

There is also a Dominant Rex, but this is very rare and does not have such a good type of woolly coat as the Recessive Rex.

The Satin was imported into the UK in 1982/83 and took a long time to establish itself. But this is an animal that, once seen, is not forgotten; they are beautiful animals. They are usually bred in any smooth-coated colour including the Long-haireds. The Satin gives the coat a very shiny effect.

## RARE AND NEW VARIETIES

In addition to the various varieties already mentioned, there are usually a few rarer varieties about. Some of these are new, for example the various longer-haired Rex, and others are older varieties that have either not proved popular or have fallen from the popular spot. The reason for the latter is usually because a more easily bred variety has come along.

A great many of these rare varieties are catered for in the UK by the Rare Varieties Cavy Club. When it was first established it only catered for two varieties, the Tortoiseshell and the Brindle. Now it has taken under its wing any new variety which is considered worthwhile.

Rare Variety cavies can be subdivided into the following categories: Standard, Guide Standard and Unstandardised. Some of these may have changed over recent times, but this is only a general guide and exact details may be obtained from the club.

When breeders of a Standard rare variety feel that they are strong enough in numbers, they may form a specialist club for that variety. Before this can take place, however, they must first apply to the club which caters for them, which is usually the RVCC, and then take their proposal, through their representative, to the British Cavy Club. If they accept and pass the proposal, then the fanciers can go ahead and form their new club.

A variety can, in the same way, be taken over by an existing club. For example the Dark-Eyed White was adopted by the English Self Cavy Club.

## TORTOISESHELLS

Rather few and far between and, although it is an old variety, it has never attained popularity. The Tort is basically a similar animal to the Tortoiseshell and White mentioned earlier, but minus the white area. It is even more difficult to breed for show than the Tort and White. It should have clearly defined patches of Red and Black.

## BRINDLES

Again, this is an old variety, but not popular; these guinea pigs should have an even intermingling of Black and Red hairs all over the

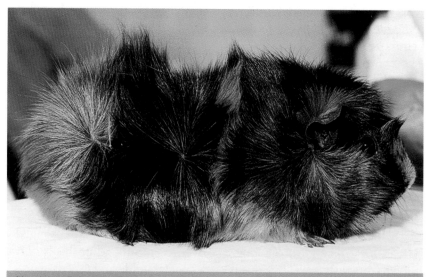

*Abysinian Brindled: An intermingling of red and black hairs.*

*Bi-coloured Agouti: Patches of two colours.*

body. It is very difficult to achieve and I feel that breeders of this variety deserve a great deal of admiration for their perseverance.

## TRI-COLOURS AND BI-COLOURS

Basically Tri-colours are patches of three-coloured animals rather like the Tort and White, but in different colours, for example: Chocolate/Cream/White, Golden Agouti/Golden/White. Bi-colours are patches of two colours like the Tort but again, in different colours, for example, Black/White, Chocolate/Cream.

## ARGENTE

This is really a Red-Eyed Agouti, the accepted colour being a Lilac-based animal with Gold ticking. Even in this variety new colours are being worked upon and I have seen a Beige-based Argente – a very beautiful animal.

## HARLEQUIN

This is yet another patchwork guinea pig. The patches are of two colours and a roaned or brindled mixture of the two, for example, Black/White/Blue Roan (sometimes known as Magpie), or Chocolate/Cream/Chocolate Cream Roan. The head markings should have half of the head one colour and the other half of the head either the other solid colour or Roan, with a straight line down the centre of the face. Feet should be alternate colours, around the body. A difficult variety to breed.

## BUFF

This is one of my favourite colours, although many people regard them as no more than dark Creams. Buff bred to Buff breed true and do not produce Creams. They are dark-eyed and can be confused with Saffron, although Saffron has red eyes.

## SAFFRON

This variety could be described as a Red-Eyed Buff, but should be rather brighter in colour than the Buff and more lemonish.

## SABLE

An extremely attractive variety that is rarely seen, it is a Chocolate on the back, and shades gradually to Beige or Cream on the belly. It can be dark, medium or light coloured.

*A Tri-coloured Texel: Three colours are discernible.*

UNIVERSITY OF LINCOLN